# Violin
# Grade 4

## Pieces
for Trinity College London exams

## 2016-2019

Published by
Trinity College London Press
trinitycollege.com

Registered in England
Company no. 09726123

Printed in England by Caligraving Ltd.

# Presto

## 3rd movt from Symphony no. 4

*Arr.* Richard Wade

J C Bach
(1735–1782)

Do not play the repeat in the exam.

poco rit.

**D. C. al Fine**

# Largo

## 1st movt from Sonata, op. 5 no. 9

Arcangelo Corelli
(1653–1713)

Do not play the repeats in the exam.

# Ceciliana and Vivace

from Sonata no. 1

Willem de Fesch
(1687–1761)

Do not play the repeats in the exam.

# Neapolitan Song

## from *Swan Lake*

*Arr.* Paul de Keyser

Pyotr Tchaikovsky
(1840–1893)

# Rondo

### from *Little School of Melody*, op. 123

*Arr.* Mary Cohen

Charles Dancla
(1817–1907)

# Smoke Gets in Your Eyes

*Arr.* Edward Huws Jones

Jerome Kern
(1885–1945)

# Leave-taking

## A Minstrel's Song

Alfred Moffat
(1863–1950)

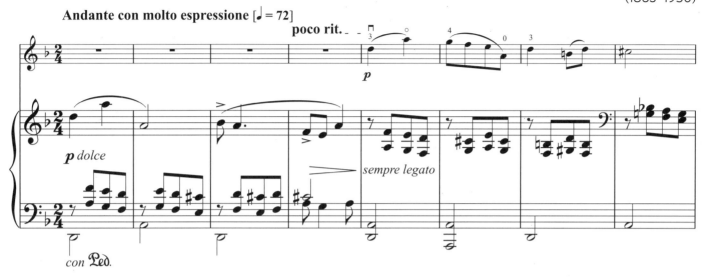

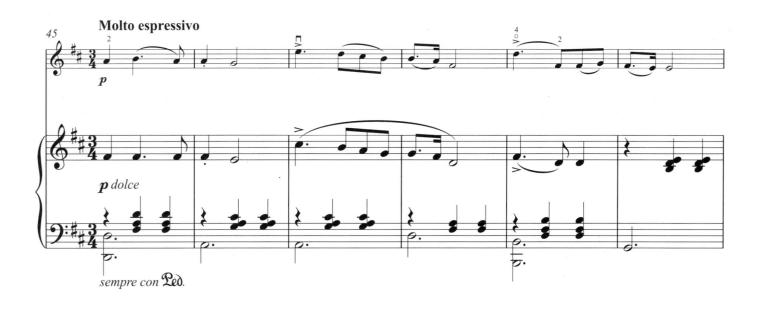

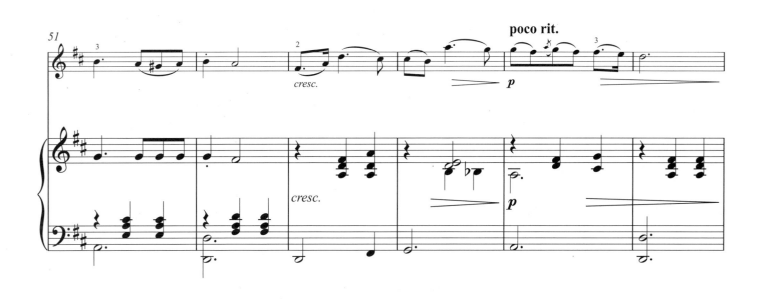

# Rustic Dance

Christopher Norton
(born 1953)

# The Fascinator

*Arr.* Edward Huws Jones

James Scott
(1885–1938)

Bracketed notes may be omitted in the exam.
Do not play the repeats in the exam, but do play the D. S. al Fine.

**D. S. al Fine**